Anna's Beautiful Blend

Written by Anna Knowles
Illustrated by Lilly Shumway

Anna's Beautiful Blend

Published by: Peas in a Pod

Text copyright © 2020 by Anna Knowles

All rights reserved. No part of this book may be used or reproduced in any manner whatsoever without specific written permission except as used in the case of brief quotations embodied in critical articles and reviews. For information, please contact Anna Knowles at annaknowlesauthor@gmail.com

ISBN: 978-1-7354978-0-8
Library of Congress Control Number:2020915039

To my mom and dad for
their infinite love and support.

My name is Anna. I'm eight years old and my dad just got married. We're going to see our new family again, and I'm feeling shy because the kids are very different from us.

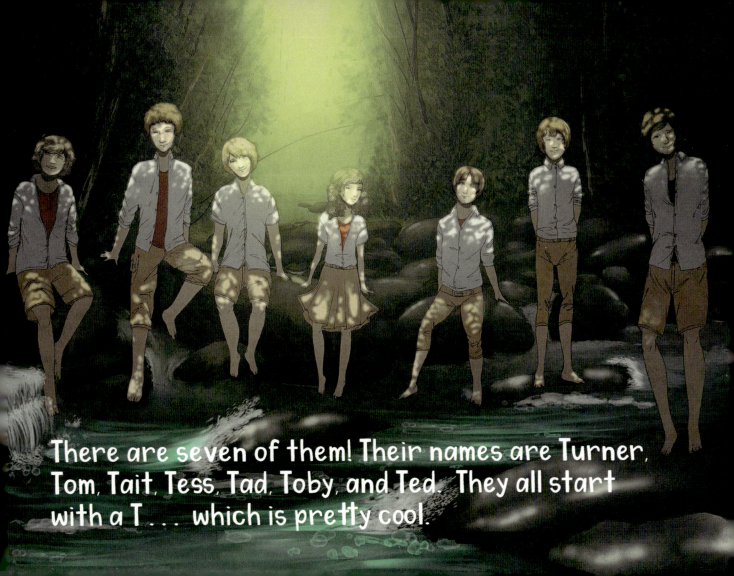

There are seven of them! Their names are Turner, Tom, Tait, Tess, Tad, Toby, and Ted. They all start with a T... which is pretty cool.

They live on a farm in the country.

We live in a house in a big city.

They ride beautiful horses.

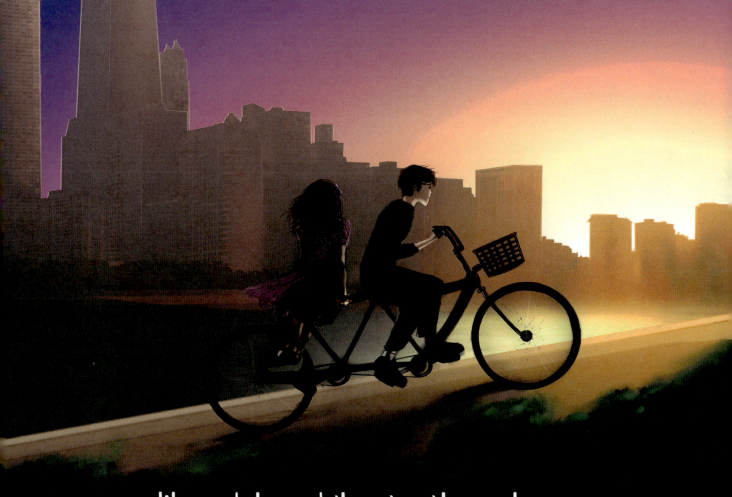

We pedal our bikes in city parks.

and we have chestnut brown.

They like to be loud.

My dad and their mom were worried.

They saw how different we were, and we didn't spend much time together.
So they came up with a plan . . .

We cleaned

and cleaned

and cleaned.

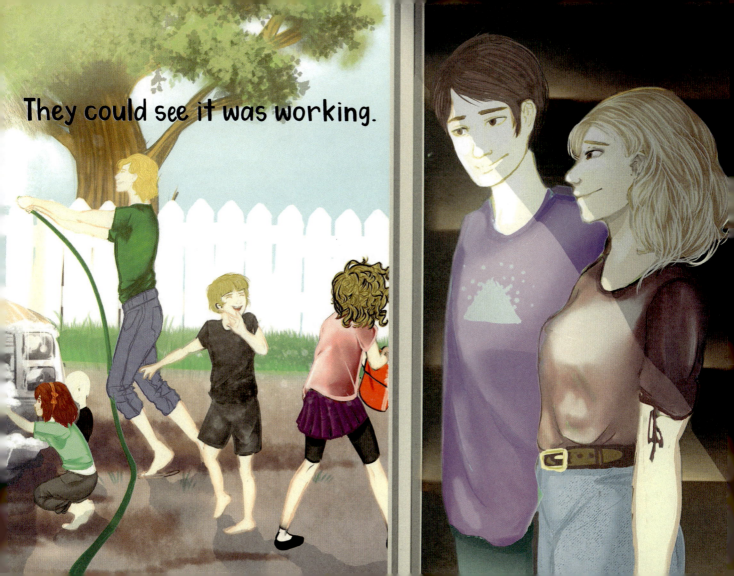

Lucy and I shared our dolls with Tess.

Tess showed us some awesome dance moves.

Toby and Tad taught Carl how to "pop a wheelie" on his bike.

Carl showed them how to play his newest video game.

After a year, our parents were happy we were getting along and becoming a family. We were surprised when they told us they were having a baby.

When the baby came, he was the cutest baby brother, and we all loved him very much.

Our differences are what made our family fun, made it beautiful. My family is a beautiful blend.

Author's Note:

I believe people with differences can unite if just given the right tools to spark conversation. In our case, they were brooms, sponges, and paint brushes.

This story came right out of the pages of my own childhood. My loving mom and dad brought two families together. They could have lectured us about getting along but instead chose a higher, more positive road. Having us do chores together was one method they used to bring us closer. I seem to remember it the most. A common ground formed between us, and from there we started to take interest in each other. Instead of dividing us, our differences made life fun and unique, and it's what made our family beautiful. There were struggles at times, but there were many more triumphs. I love my family and my childhood. I wouldn't change a thing about it or the people in it.

About the Author:

Anna Knowles has an Elementary Education degree. She loved reading her favorite picture books to her students. She grew up mostly in the Chicago area but now lives in Colorado with her husband and three children. She loves to travel with her husband and work on family history with her Dad. One of her greatest adventures was visiting Lettomanoppello, Italy, where she learned about her ancestors and slept under the same stars. *Anna's Beautiful Blend* is her debut illustrated children's book.

About the Illustrator:

Twenty-year-old, Lilly Shumway is a freelance artist, born in Las Vegas, Nevada, and raised in Parker, Colorado. Though new and inexperienced, she is passionate and earnest about her work. Lilly believes the world is a beautiful and wondrous place and strives to revere it in each of her pieces. She specializes in digital and traditional art.

Made in the USA
Middletown, DE
01 December 2021